Finger of Fury

Finger of Fury

A Book of Verse

Fredrick Burns

authorHOUSE®

AuthorHouse™
1663 Liberty Drive
Bloomington, IN 47403
www.authorhouse.com
Phone: 1-800-839-8640

Published by AuthorHouse   01/25/2013

ISBN: 978-1-4670-3552-1 (sc)
ISBN: 978-1-4670-3551-4 (e)

Library of Congress Control Number: 2011916629

CONTENTS

PARTY TWISTER

it was 2am and the party was a rockin'
i was feeling fine 'til Joe started talkin'
a tornado's touched down about a mile from here
let's head for the cellar and bring the beer!

well i went outside and what did i see?
a mean lookin' twister bearin' down on me
it hopped to the left and skipped to the right
i could only stare at the incredible sight

the wind was a screamin' and i heard it say
i'm lookin' for a party so get outta my way!
oh, i'm a bad old twister i'm the Finger of Fury
a headin' cross country as judge and jury!

i threw my beer and it sucked it right in
then the twister hit me with a bottle of gin
it knocked me out and i fell to the ground
a few minutes later i heard a creakin' sound

the door to my basement was all i could see
it swung open and my friends looked at me
we smiled at each other and shed a few tears
then cursed that old twister lookin' for beers

THE CEO

standing in the shadow
of a corporate glass tower
a man without expression
asks me for change

i give him a dollar
and he looks skyward
mockingly declaring
that he'd been a CEO

i had a big office
wore a suit of blue
i lived to make profits
off people like you
i rode in a limo
drank French champagne
shook hands with the President
he knew me by name

i was brash and i was bold
never would I be undersold
i bought up companies
that were on their knees
and dreamed of a monopoly
holding all the keys

i had a home theatre
with a big screen TV
images larger than life
business news all about me

then
that child in Africa
wearing combats
holding one of my weapons
pulling the trigger
all innocence lost

FRIENDS

sitting with you
by the crackling fire
i gaze upon the mountains
their snow-capped peaks
awash in crimson
by the setting sun
and i reflect
upon the perfect day
we have just shared
our early morning walk
along the beach
driving country roads
in my vintage car
hiking along trails
in the lush rainforest
sharing ice cream
on the hot afternoon
and playing frisbee
at a neighbour's barbecue
looking into your warm eyes
i smile softly
and say thank-you friend
your tail wagging happily
in agreement

ONCE A CHILD

watching
children at play
in a cardboard box
laughing
singing
so carefree
i shed a tear
an image recalled
under a bridge
in a cardboard box
an old man
once a child

DREAMS

chasing rainbows
catching stars
building castles
up in the sky
painting pictures
weaving dreams
making wings
on which to fly
counting years
smiling through tears
shed from chains
of bondage

THE NURSERY MAN

driving by my friend's house
i had to stop and say
i love your shrubs and flowers
they really make my day

thank you for the compliment
but these I did not grow
please join me in the kitchen
i have something else to show

we sat down at the table
to share a pot of tea
while admiring her Skimmia
from the land of Zeider Zee

i bought them from dear Eellco
a man who i call 'Dutch'
when it comes to growing flowers
he has a magic touch

gardening is his passion
you can see it in his eyes
he has a reverence for the Earth
and Nature's many skies

you can find his nursery
down on Parker Lane
there you'll see him working
and singing in the rain

BIRDSONG

the chickadee
could be heard
greeting a new morn
what peace is found
in this little bird's song
and in its simplicity
the apparent chaos of life
is gently washed away

GENESIS

sitting by a waterfall
shrouded in mist
of ancient stars
a dying man
is caressed
by gentle breezes
remnants
of galactic storms
his last breath
giving birth
to a distant moon

SEASONS

life
seasons
in change
old growth
replaced
by new
stagnation
death
but fallacy

A WISH

i cast a wish
upon the moonlit river
it dances
i watch
it sings
i listen
it vanishes
i can only hope

FORGIVENESS

broken promises
shattered dreams
life's not always
as it seems
heart so cold
with truths untold
seeks forgiveness
but from whom?

FLYING

on wounded wing
i fly
my heart
heavy as the moist air
tears
falling
like acid rain
yet i fly

STORM

in troubled times
bend like a tree
in a storm
once having passed
brings sunshine
and birds
to fill your life
with song

SOCIO-SURVIVAL

move
like a deer
in the forest
step
stop
look
listen
repeat

BORDERS

standing
on the surface
of the moon
the spaceman
saw no borders
upon the earth
and unheard
were voices
of intolerance

NEEDING YOU

it's nice
to be needed
hospitals
need patients
jails
need criminals
welfare
needs recipients
caution
vested interest

NEW HORIZON

fallen leaf
upon silver stream
riding current
dare to dream
of distant delta
open seas
an horizon
yet unclaimed

HAPPY BIRTHDAY

birthdays come and go
marking passage
of your time
age a number
finite
incomprehensible
to an infinite soul

THE BUTTERCUP

waiting
at a bus stop
his thoughts shift
scattered pieces
bombs falling
mills polluting
muggers killing
children crying
homeless begging
farmers quitting
addicts dying
families breaking
ad nauseum
the images interrupted
a single buttercup
growing through a crack
in the sidewalk
its spirit whispering
despite the drudgery
the world is still
a place of beauty

TODAY

cross the threshold
of tomorrow
by living today
dwell not on the past
for it will occupy your soul
with no room for the present
and a future left wanting

THE HAUNTING

dying alone
i eventually crossed
the great divide
between life and death
and saw strangers
in my little house
rummaging through my things
all respect tossed aside
such a scene
haunting me
forever

dying alone
i was laid to rest
against my wishes
in a plain pine box
covered with earth
as an unknown pastor
delivered a generic eulogy
to a gathering of none
such a scene
haunting me
forever

dying alone
i was left waiting
with a glimmer of joy
for angels or St. Peter
maybe the pre-deceased
and there i remained
in the freezing void
no light no sound no hope
such a scene
haunting me
forever

A NATION'S BIRTHDAY

they show us smiling faces
but only certain places
hoping we'll stay blind
without the will to find
the cold and dark reality
a million hungry children
a million more to come
we can hear them crying
but nothing's ever done
women bruised
criticized and abused
First Nations still neglected
another liar gets elected

ELECTION YEAR

my name is Joe
i'm your candidate
i shake your hand
you take the bait
i flash a smile
and look you in the eye
you smile back
never thinking i would lie
my chances of winning
may be remote
so i'll do anything
to get your vote
oh, it's another election year
i tell you what you want to hear
i'll treat you like a flock of sheep
making promises i'll never keep
making promises i'll never keep

THE SENTENCE

the State demanded restitution
the judge then ordered execution
the people wanted to see him die
give him the chair and let him fry
collectively they've sealed his fate
but is this justice or is it hate?

FOOTSTEPS

footsteps on the back porch
his daddy has come home
he cringes beneath the covers
feeling all alone
holding onto Teddy
he sees the kitchen light
mother's up to greet him
for yet another fight
fist upon the table
a slap across the face
out you lousy drunk
get off my bloody case
voices raised in anger
a shout and then a scream
he closes his eyes so very tight
and prays it's just a dream

CHOICES

down Main street
in Victory Park
home to pigeons
and derelicts
lights flash
a crowd gathers
paramedics
work in vain
as death permeates
the frigid morning air

staring
at the shrouded body
being removed
from the scene
the curious murmer
poor soul
rest in peace
only to be silenced
by a voice
on the chilling wind

show me no sorrow
for i have chosen
to abuse my family
live life in a bottle
share dirty needles
and die in the cold
now mark these words
it is never to late
to still become
what you might have been

THE SHOEMAKER

he awakens
on his tenth birthday
before the rising sun
sliding past his brothers
as grandfather sleeps
with a watchful eye

for lack of kindling
he skips his cup of tea
and heads barefoot
out into the rain
the cold mud oozing
between his toes

he hastens to board
and antiquated bus
which rumbles along
its belching tailpipe
leaking diesel fumes
into the crowded coach

the mood is somber
no one speaks
in this daily nightmare
all eyes watching
for the colossal gates
like those at the prison

entering the compound
mechanical monsters
can already be heard
instruments of fear
playing a symphony
of exploitation and profit

marched in like soldiers
he will train a new kid
at his workstation
the adjacent unattended
as yesterday a young girl
severed three fingers

under constant threat
of a foreman's baton
and permanent dismissal
he works feverishly
tracing cutting stitching
one hundred soles today

his hands bruised and sore
he stares unconsciously
at countless piles
of finished shoes
too exhausted to think
about all the people
who can afford them

THE SALESMAN

on a golf course
a setting so serene
two men at play
one asks
what do you do?
i sell hardware
computers?
no
building supplies?
military
guns and bombs?
we call it hardware
feel guilty?'
sometimes
why not quit?
good money

TEARS

make love
not war
my heart
wants to sing
if it should cry
let it shed
only tears of joy

THE DANCER

she dances
swaying
golden wheat
caressed
by gentle breeze
taking flight
she soars
landing softly
as a butterfly
upon a flower

CHANGE

wind
whispering words
of wisdom
fear not change
a gift
to be cherished
designed
especially for you

LIFE

life
a journey
through time
like a river
in a valley
swift rapids
steep waterfalls
calm pools
lazy meanders
a course uncertain

CROSSFIRE

somewhere on the border
two armies exchanged fire
a bloody round of violence
fuelled by senseless ire
a young boy lay dying
he didn't have chance
caught in the crossfire
a victim of circumstance
born into endless conflict
he was exposed to hate
now in his shortened life
he met this tragic fate
caught in the crossfire
pinned against a wall
the young boy lay dying
a lesson for us all

20/20

stricken
with a dark cancer
too weak for a knife
she was bombarded
with invisible waves
bringing not recovery
but life-taking nausea
now with hindsight
the pundits' warning
becomes quite clear
should the big one
be dropped upon us
that same sickness
shall be our own demise

CAMPING

by shimmering moon
golden leaves flutter
in Autumn breeze
sparkling stars
in transparent sky
smell of canvass tenting
cocooned
in our sleeping bags
we whisper
breaking silence
of the deep woods
the oneness
of the moment
shared
you
me
Mother Earth

SENSES

rain falling lightly upon my head
wind blowing softly in my ear
waves lapping gently against my feet
your touch
your voice
your kiss

DESTINY

sailing
on my ship
winds carry me
across the ocean
to my destiny
there she waits
with hope
desire
and love
a candle in the night

MYSTERY

whose lips are these
that kiss me tenderly
in my dream?
she makes me quiver
with a velvet touch
yet dissolves my fears
with a whisper
whose heart beats
as one with mine?
oh that i may live
long enough to know

MAGIC

you are the first star
i see at night
when i wish i may
i wish i might
you are the genie
in the bottle
i found on the beach
you are the dream
that chased away
my nightmare
i now believe
in magic

SENIOR LOVE

we still speak of our destiny
a journey hand in hand
and we walk along a moonlit beach
to write i love you in the sand
we make sweet love with our eyes
like we did in years gone by
our hearts still beat strong as one
and they will until we die
i'd never have known such happiness
which has often brought me to tears
if it weren't for the precious love
you've given all these years

FALLING STARS

twilight came
every so slowly
the first star
i named after you
upon your cheek
teardrops
falling stars
in their own way
love is light

SHADOWS

throwing shadows
at you
in a darkened room
looking for a crack
in the impenetrable wall
that imprisons your soul

THE TRIP

today i won a trip for two
to an island in the sun
but now that i'm all alone
it wouldn't be much fun
a dear friend tried to tell me
there'd be ladies on the beach
but ever since my sweetheart died
love's been out of reach
if there ever was a journey
on which i'd want to go
it would be to see my angel
to say i love her so

RAIN ART

raindrops
drawing lines
on my window
no pattern discerned
etchings
random
as my thoughts
in your absence

TRUE LOVE

true love
a grain of sand
to be found
in the desert
a task
so daunting
the grain
made elusive
by the wind
perhaps
blown to you
yet unknowingly
brushed away

THE WALL

oh, the wall
that god-forsaken wall
built by your heart
insurmountable
indestructible
a monument
to your incertitudes

COLD TRUTH

opening the door
to your heart
you let me in
there we shared
precious moments
and then you left
i waited patiently
for your return
as the warm fire
slowly reduced itself
to a few dying embers
in the darkness
i heard wind chimes
speaking of a truth
one as bitter
as the winter wind

THE VOYAGE

on course
with compass true
yet my craft drifts
under thirsting sky
a gull sleeps
on the stern
reluctant to fly
in the still air
patiently i wait
half-delirious
from the blazing sun
then from the west
a whisper
upon your breath
my sails billow
the placid waters
now broken
by determined bow

NO SORROW

press your sweet lips
against my cheek
whisper those words
i have longed to hear
trepid as they have been
in time i have learned
there's no sorrow greater
than your absence

DESERT OF LOVE

beaten
by searing winds
and scorching sun
choking
on swirling sands
i was lost
in the desert
of love
but in you
i found an oasis
sweet kisses
wetting
my parched lips
gentle caresses
soothing
a burning skin
my live saved
by eternal love

THE FOUNTAIN

i drink no more
from your fountain
of love
its waters
now tainted
leave a bitter taste
upon my lips

THE BOOK

like a book
you place me
upon a shelf
to be read
at your leisure
but over time
with fading ink
i am gone

SOLITUDE

standing alone
in a meadow
under the cover
of darkness
i quiver
my senses heightened
your sweet fragrance
in the flowers
bright eyes
amongst the stars
and gentle voice
upon the wind

THOUGHTS OF YOU

thoughts of you
warm my heart
on the coldest day
they light my path
on the darkest night
and shelter my soul
from the fiercest storm
thoughts of you
i treasure

ANTICIPATION

loving words
from your lips
gentle touch
upon my cheek
warm smile
across your face
with sweet anticipation
i wait
frozen in time
one moment
an eternity

LOVE

love
is a verb
transitive
love someone
love something
be loved
without condition
now

INCOMPARABLE

he kneels
before her
hand extended
a yellow rose
of friendship
her beauty
rare as diamonds
more so
the gems
incomparable
to the brilliance
of her soul

H2O

your love
is like spring water
refreshing my spirit
purifying my heart
satisfying my thirst
for life

TRUE WEALTH

glittering gold
shining silver
worthless scrap
compared to the value
i place on your love
never poor
never wanting
i'm rich beyond my dreams

HARMONY

a subtle gesture
words unspoken
our souls connect
in perfect harmony

WONDER LOVE

the moon is made of silver
and the sun is made of gold
the stars are really diamonds
so i have been told
but none can match your beauty
those objects up above
compared to what i see in you
that's the wonder of your love

TOGETHER

time and distance
barriers between us
yet take comfort
we stand on the same Earth
read the same stars
and feel the same sun
together

IMAGINATION

she lights a candle
to set the mood
though he remains
in darkness
the soft music
felt but not heard
he imagines her
a gentle caress
kisses tender
scent of wildflower
her very presence
warming his heart
touching his soul

Fredrick Burns

LOVE CYCLE

love
like a stream
has no beginning
no end
it flows
evaporates
flows again
a cycle
everlasting

REFLECTIONS

strolling with you
beside a stream
our reflections
reveal our oneness
more than we can se
in ourselves

MISSING YOU

longing for your voice
i listen to the wind
but hear just the silence
of my deep sorrow
longing for your scent
i pick a garden rose
but sense only pain
as a thorn pierces my soul
longing for your touch
i stand in the Spring rain
but fall numb from the cold
in the reality of loneliness